PRAISE FOR STEVEN CRAMER'S POETRY

The World Book (1992)

"Cramer's poems fight sentiment with our only available weapons: knowledge and integrity."

—Ploughshares

Dialogue for the Left and Right Hand (1997)

"Cramer's narrative and dramatic poems are intelligent and polished. While much contemporary poetry resembles blocks of prose chopped arbitrarily into lines, his graceful free verse all but scans. Nor does refinement damp urgency or inventiveness. Some of his memories are wrenching . . . and his similes range from adroit to dazzling."

—Poetry

Goodbye to the Orchard (2004)

"Steven Cramer's fourth book . . . provides page after page of graceful inquisition and controlled musicality."

—Harvard Review

Clangings (2012)

"Steven Cramer, in his fifth collection, employs an innovative strategy, opening himself to the space outside of language by pushing up against its limitations. *Clangings* is a restless, ambitious enterprise."

—Poets' Quarterly

Listen (2020)

"In his sixth collection . . . Cramer . . . looks at and through the fogs of memory and depression [and] tries to distill a "bedlam of thought." He is, by turns, matter of fact, nailing the sometimes-funny sometimes-sad absurdity of the world."

—Boston Globe

Departures from Rilke **(2023)**

"In this fascinating collection, Steven Cramer's seventh, the prize-winning poet and essayist . . . vaults Rilke's work over the intervening century and delivers a selection of poems that are more modern than their originals yet retain Rilke's intoxicating combination of ethereality and physicality."

—*Harvard Review*

ALSO BY STEVEN CRAMER

Departures from Rilke (2023)

Listen (2020)

Clangings (2012)

Goodbye to the Orchard (2004)

Dialogue for the Left and Right Hand (1997)

The World Book (1992)

The Eye That Desires to Look Upward (1987)

As If

Variations on Enrique Anderson-Imbert

Steven Cramer

LILY POETRY REVIEW BOOKS

Copyright © 2025 by Steven Cramer
Published by Lily Poetry Review Books
223 Winter Street
Whitman, MA 02382

https://lilypoetryreview.blog/

ISBN: 978-1-957755-60-1

Cover art: Francisco Goya, *A Way of Flying:* Artist's proof, etching and drypoint,
collection of Lázaro Galdiano Museum, Madrid

The size of the image is very important to the emotion.

—Alfred Hitchcock

CONTENTS

AUTHOR'S NOTE

I owe these variations to a search committee I served on, years ago, for an assistant professor in creative writing. The candidate—who turned out to be our top pick and turned us down—began his presentation by writing the following twenty-eight words on the blackboard:

> TRAP
>
> After the last birds died the cage took off from the patio and began flying toward heaven. "It's coming to ask our forgiveness," thought the unwary angels.

None in our audience of five knew about the Argentine writer Enrique Anderson-Imbert (1910-2000), author of this astonishing example of his "microcuentos," perfectly translated by Isabel Reade. We asked the candidate to pause so we could copy it down.

Appetite whetted, I searched out other Englished microcuentos. Despite their many arresting, fabulist scenarios, none that I found lived up to Reade's translation of "Trap"—which is prose that feels like a poem. The other microcuentos, at least in English, were prose that felt prosaic. They didn't have what poetry can't do without: the sense of something *palpably left unsaid.* Was Anderson-Imbert, then, a particularly maltreated victim of his translators, or a curious epitome of the one-hit wonder?

Lacking Spanish, I couldn't pursue those questions. Instead, the interventionist in me tried coaching some of Anderson-Imbert's prose fables into verse, hopeful that the infrastructures of stanza and line— and the junctures between lines and stanzas—could create spaces for the spaced-out logic at the hearts of these little stories.

1

AGORAPHOBIA

Bathed, shaved, dressed,

"let's go out for a walk,"

he said into his mirror—

no, the mirror answered.

AS IF

When he got home in the very early morning,
the dark in his house darker than outside dark,

he took off his shoes before climbing the stairs.
But was this his house? Entering the bedroom,

who might he find asleep and breathing in his bed,
dreaming of taking his shoes off, and of climbing

the stairs to his bedroom, waking and turning
on the lamp, hearing soft footfalls on the stairs?

BACK HOME

He finds in his jacket pocket
a postcard he can't remember,

addressed to him but unsigned,
no postmark. *Wish you were still*

with me, love—in an unknown hand.
Palms indicate a southern resort.

Maybe someone passing him
as he stood on a street corner

mistook him for a mailbox.
Maybe it wasn't a mistake.

BREAKING THE FOURTH WALL

Our two-foot-tall host called it his first milk tooth,
but a canine the size of a tusk hung on his wall.

He must have been born a giant, shrinking each year.
His voice like a music box ballerina, he guided us

along his neighborhood's streets: each one a waterway
after the monsoons. "Next visit, bring microscopes,"

he told us. Then he dove in. "Pretty good swimmer,"
someone observed, "but isn't it 'dived,' not 'dove?'"

BULL

A two-horned unicorn charged toward the girl,
its pace and gait like a bull's, its torso not so
much so, more like a . . . like . . . like . . . oh,
I don't know.

        "But I know you," said the girl,
her smirk wide as the rusted tines of a rake.
"Think I'm such a dolt that I'd take a joy ride
on your horns? Besides, one of them's fake,
you metaphor you."

           With nowhere to hide
but inside his myth, a fairytale found out now,
for the first time the unicorn felt recognized
as the bull he always knew he was, and bowed.

ELSEWHERE

Whenever the judge took a break from his courtroom,
he passed the same beggar: face loose as hung washing,

right eye looking heavenward, clear as wisdom;
left fixed on the face of Satan. Satan, his assassin. . .

As always, the judge fled, phoned his clerk, ordering
the beggar put to death by beheading. But elsewhere

in the multiverse, the beggar housed and employed,
the judge never saw him, neither then nor then again,

and walked back to his bench to do more judging.
Meanwhile, the clerk's still searching for the beggar,

but after the beggar's red-eye lands in San Francisco,
he nabs him in the graveyard behind Mission Dolores,

my favorite site from Hitchcock's *Vertigo*—oh green
dream of a film, of love dragged back from the dead!—

and beheads him. Body down a well, head in a sack,
the clerk brings this job well done back to his boss.

Elsewhere, the judge screams: *what have you done?*
Elsewhere, the world's beautiful if I close my eyes.

THE EYE THAT DESIRES TO
LOOK UPWARD

When my father lay dying in the hospital,
he waved a copy of my first book of poems

at every doctor, nurse, and orderly he met,
I'm told. "Look! My son wrote a book!"

The last time he called me, he spoke
to my machine from Intensive Care.

Barely a rumor of death in his voice,
I erased it with the others on the tape.

Next morning he died, so I never learned
what poems from my first book he read,

if any. Did he read the one about him,
that one in which the speaker lies down

and plays dead next to his dead body?
Later on the night he phoned, he'd go

in and out of consciousness. At worst,
maybe he hallucinated reading the poem.

Hallucinated: hard word to fit into a poem
about a father's death. So many syllables. . .

I hope he didn't read it. Thirty-six years,
and still I hope he never read that poem.

FRIENDSHIP

David swore David to secrecy.
"I'll be silent as a grave," said David;

thus began a devoted friendship—
David always talking, but David

going quieter, then silent, not
like a grave, but in fact a grave,

two angels of grief on the stone.

HISTORY

His travel grant came through, so where should he go?
The Roaring 20s? The Enlightenment? The Renaissance?

Because he just turned forty, the Middle Ages maybe?
The morning suddenly went dark. When he looked up,

he expected to see clouds, with a remote hint of thunder.
Instead, he saw a giant hand draw back behind the sky,

as if unsure how to move on history's chessboard: queen,
bishop, knight, rook, pawn? Or stay unmoved like the king?

THE HOLE OF BABYLON

Millennia ago, in Babylon, in a wall
between two mud-brick houses, first

the hole turned into a mouth, then an ear;
finally, at nightfall, it narrowed to an eye.

The hole looked to the right, to the left,
but the lovers it hoped for didn't show.

Without ears, it listened for footsteps
fruitlessly; and no mouths whispered.

Millennia of waiting, and still no lovers—
no Pyramus, no Thisbe, just to name

two among the more doomed ones.
Millennia of spiders constructing webs.

ICARUS

Dad didn't get my imagination
whenever I chirruped birdsongs,

broke into a trot during our walks,
or made like a whale vacuuming krill.

The last time we flew together,
I *wanted* the sun to melt the wax

fastening wings to my shoulders.
To feel how a fish breathes water,

I wanted to plunge into the sea.

LAST WORDS OF THE NARCISSIST

"This comes from the top,"
his guardian angel warned—

"anyone who says *stupid* dies."
"Just who you calling *stupid?*"

THE MAP

In the back of a drawer, I found a map of my city.
At first, I didn't know what the many X's meant,

then I remembered: they marked spots where I lost
those things I never admitted I loved.   Who cared

so much for me, or so little, that they'd leave me
this map I might or might not find? Map in hand,

I scoured the city. What a waste! Any valuables—
umbrella, pen, wallet, watch, some gloves, a knife—

street thieves must have swiped; the worthless stuff—
a glasses wipe, a Band-Aid™—rain had flushed away.

Ready to go home, I looked up: on a stone bench
just outside the park, maybe weeping, as if missing

someone loved, sat the one I'd arrived too late for.

PARADE

His girlfriend stabbed him in the neck.
Instead of pulling out the knife, he let it

take root as part of his life. More than that,
it remade his life from the day of his birth,

even from the night he was conceived—
its cylindrical hilt erect over a shoulder blade,

so his body took on greater heft, less flesh
than metal. At last, he felt like a man!—

and better yet, worth more looks than one.
Women, curbside, watched for him to pass;

the force of their held breath gave him heart,
or was that just heat off the summer street?

Name any man who's not a parade of one.

PER AGREEMENT

Each boy assembling in the lot
brought a different kind of stick—

a lance, mop handle, flagpole,
stilts: a woodland of stiff limbs

over their heads. The last boy
arrived just in time on crutches,

toothpick poking from his lips.

SIN

Richard was both lazy and bad—
one flaw often ruling out the other.

When he lay on his couch all day,
he couldn't do bad things; but lying,

stealing, insulting his wife, or worse,
put him out. Then back to his couch.

One morning, as he rode the subway
from the center of his city to his stop,

a man entered and sat next to him.
"Excuse me, what station do I take

to go to . . ."—naming a landmark
in the faltering accent of a foreigner.

"Well," Richard answered the air,
"just get out at the station after mine."

Shit, Richard thought, I did some good.
Of course, I could choose to get off

a stop before or a stop after mine,
just to be sure I've worsened his life.

But which of those two wrong stops
requires the longer walk to my couch?

The train kept going, he kept thinking:
is there any sin worse than indecision?

THANK YOU

Walking in my city after work,
I felt a heart attack come on,

and began falling to my knees.
I could hear but couldn't see

whoever dashed from the dark
storefront, rushed toward me,

and lifted me back to my feet.
"Thank you," I began to say,

sensing the stranger straighten,
before a grip, its touch white

as hollow bone, bore me off.

THREE THIRTY-THREE A.M.

I woke up in a jealous sweat
from my lover and best friend

fucking in my dream. Like a coal
red from hell, this thought hissed:

if my own dreams cheat on me,
what worse crimes lie beside me?

TWO GHOSTS

One summer night I lay down under a yew tree.
Nearly asleep, I heard what I thought was a cow,
its moo continuous, rusty, like a groaning hinge.

At the farthest edge of the field, too dark to see,
a door creaked open and out he came, head aglow.
"Excuse me," he said, wisps of red and blue flame

lighting me up as I stood. "Who in hell are you?"
I asked, my voice so dry it also groaned a little.
"Sorry. My mistake," he said. "What do you want?"

"Nothing. My bad. But this is the other world,
isn't it?" "What do you mean: 'the other world?'"
I lay back down—"anyway, no. This is the world."

UNTITLED

A washed-up author chose to kill himself,
parking a loaded gun next to his laptop.

Words, like breath slapped into a newborn,
thrived, grew, and bore the last great book

his suicide turned into an instant bestseller.

THE WAY THE PSYCHOPATH SAW IT

The psychopath felt no guilt, least of all
before God. In fact, he resented God
who must have hoarded the Universe
before deigning to create the world.
No more chaos! From now on cosmos.

But if He made all things, why guilt-
trip Adam and Eve for Original Sin?—
a measly sin at that—and what kind
of Eden dies from just a bite of fruit?
About all the sin that followed: so what?

We sin due to God's will, not despite it,
since nothing happens not by God's will.
Instead, God Himself sins against Himself
—humanity permitting. What makes God
punish Himself? Making us: His original sin.

NOTES AND SOURCES

Anderson-Imbert's collections of microcuentos include *The Cheshire Cat* (1965), *The Grimoire* (1969), and *The Swindler Retires* (1969). The sources in English for my variations were published in *Cage with Only One Side,* translated by Isabel Reade (West Coast Poetry Review, 1974); *Woven on the Loom of Time,* translated by Carleton Vail and Pamela Edwards-Mondragón (University of Texas Press, 1990); and *Short Stories by Enrique Anderson-Imbert* (2006-2014), translated by Armand F. Baker (https://armandfbaker.github.io/anderson_imbert. html). With two exceptions, the poems' titles are mine.

From *The Cheshire Cat*
Agoraphobia: from "The Pomegranate"
As If: "Spiral"
Back Home: from "Hints of What Is Possible"
Bull: "The Unicorn"
Elsewhere: "Cross Eyed"
The Eye That Desires to Look Upward: from "Diary"
Friendship: from "The Pomegranate"
History: from "The Pomegranate"
The Hole of Babylon: from "The Pomegranate"
Icarus: "Icarus"
The Map: from "Relationships"
Parade: from "The Pomegranate"
Per Agreement: from "The Pomegranate"
Sin: "Doubt"
Thank You: from "Death"
Untitled: from "The Pomegranate"
The Way the Psychopath Saw It: from "The Gods"

From *The Grimoire*
Breaking the Fourth Wall: "Microscopy"
Last Words of The Narcissist: "Taboo"
Two Ghosts: "The Two Ghosts"

From *The Swindler Retires*
Three Thirty-Three A.M.: "Jealousy"

ACKNOWLEDGMENTS

Thanks to the editors of the following periodicals where some of these poems first appeared:

Lily Poetry Review: "Agoraphobia," "Back Home," "Breaking the Fourth Wall," "Bull," "Friendship"; *Ocean State Review*: "The Hole of Babylon"; *Plume:* "The Eye That Desires to Look Upward," "Two Ghosts"; *Red Letter Poetry:* "History," "Icarus"

As always, my love and gratitude to Teresa Cader and Joyce Peseroff, and a special thanks to Eileen Cleary and Martha McCollough at Lily Poetry Review Books.

ABOUT THE AUTHOR

As If: Variations on Enrique Anderson-Imbert is Steven Cramer's first chapbook. His previous seven books are *The Eye that Desires to Look Upward* (Galileo Press, 1987); *The World Book* (Copper Beech Press, 1992); *Dialogue for the Left and Right Hand* (Lumen Editions/Brookline Books, 1997); *Goodbye to the Orchard* (Sarabande Books, 2004)— winner of the 2005 Sheila Motton Prize from the New England Poetry Club and named a 2005 Honor Book in Poetry by the Massachusetts Center for the Book—*Clangings* (Sarabande Books, 2012); *Listen* (MadHat Press, 2020), long-listed as a "must read" by the Massachusetts Center for the Book; and *Departures from Rilke* (Arrowsmith Press, 2023). His poems and reviews have appeared in *The Atlantic Monthly, Field, Kenyon Review, The Nation, The New Republic, The Paris Review, Ploughshares, Poetry,* and other journals. His work is represented in anthologies such as *The Autumn House Anthology of Contemporary American Poetry* (Autumn House Press, 2005 and 2011), *The Book of Villanelles* (Knopf Everyman's Library Pocket Poets Series, 2012), and *The POETRY Anthology, 1912-2002* (Ivan R. Dee, 2002). He has also written essays for *Simply Lasting: Writers on Jane Kenyon* (Graywolf Press, 2005); *Touchstones: American Poets on a Favorite Poem* (Middlebury College Press, 1996); and *Until Everything Is Continuous Again: American Poets on the Recent Work of W.S. Merwin* (WordFarm, 2012). Recipient of fellowships from the Massachusetts Cultural Council and the National Endowment for the Arts, he has taught literature and writing at Bennington College, Boston University, M.I.T., and Tufts University; and he founded the Low-Residency MFA Program in Creative Writing at Lesley University in Cambridge, Massachusetts.